Fortune's Bones

THE MANUMISSION REQUIEM

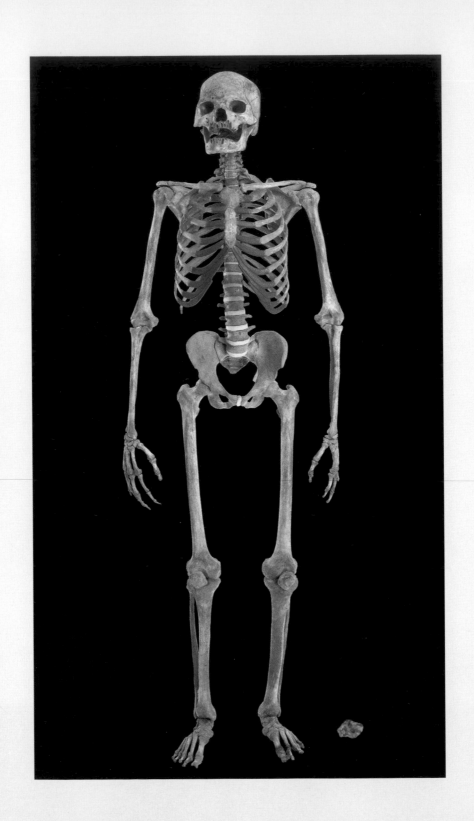

Fortune's Bones

THE MANUMISSION REQUIEM

Marilyn Nelson

Notes and annotations by
Pamela Espeland

FRONT STREET
Asheville, North Carolina

WE GRATEFULLY ACKNOWLEDGE
THE CONNECTICUT COMMISSION ON THE ARTS AND
THE MATTATUCK MUSEUM OF WATERBURY, CONNECTICUT,
WHOSE GENEROSITY AND COOPERATION
MADE THE PROJECT POSSIBLE.

Library of Congress Cataloging-in-Publication Data

Nelson, Marilyn
Fortune's bones : the manumission requiem / Marilyn Nelson.–1st ed.
p. cm.
Includes bibliographical references (p.).
ISBN 1-932425-12-8 (alk. paper)
1. Slaves–Poetry. 2. Slavery–Poetry. 3. Connecticut–Poetry.
4. African Americans—Poetry. 5. Young adult poetry, American. I. Title.
PS 3573.A4795F64 2004
811'.54-dc22   2004046917

Fortune's Bones

THE MANUMISSION REQUIEM

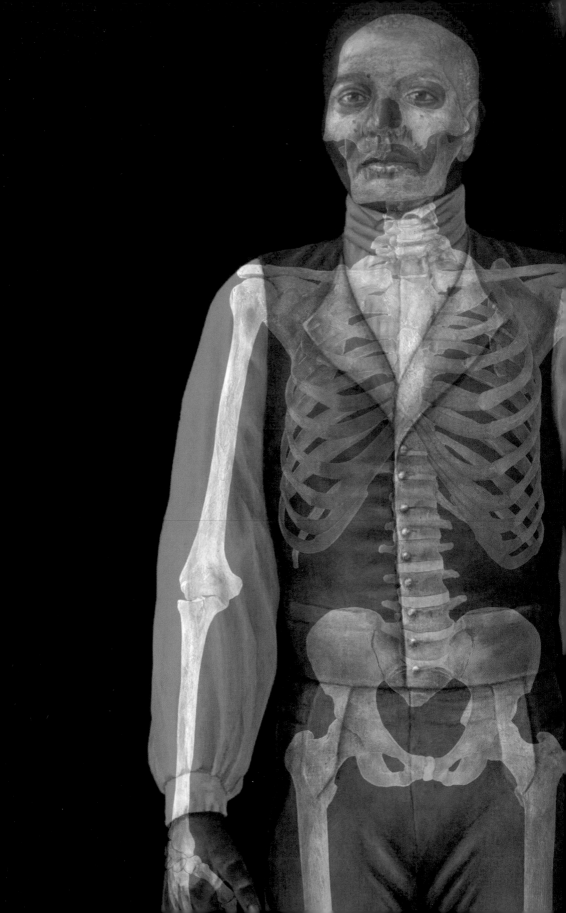

Contents

Preliminary score for
The Manumission Requiem
by Dr. Ysaye M. Barnwell

Manumission: The formal release of someone who has been a slave.

From the Latin words *manus* (hand) and *mittere* (to release, let go, or send). Literally "to release the hand of authority."

Slave owners could choose to free their slaves. Sometimes slaves were freed if they converted to their masters' religion.

Requiem: Words and music written to honor the dead.

The first word of the Introit (first part) of the Mass for the Dead (*missa pro defunctis*): *"Requiem aeternam dona eis, Domine: et lux perpetua luceat eis ..."* ("Give them eternal rest, O Lord, and let perpetual light shine upon them ...")

A musical setting of the requiem mass; a musical composition in honor of someone who has died.

Famous requiems have been written by Wolfgang Amadeus Mozart, Hector Berlioz, Gabriel Fauré, and Benjamin Britten, to name a few. Music for *The Manumission Requiem* has been composed by Dr. Ysaye M. Barnwell.

The Manumission Requiem: Written to honor a slave named Fortune, freed from slavery by death.

Although Fortune was baptized in St. John's Episcopal Church in Waterbury, Connecticut, in 1797, conversion did not make slaves free in that state after 1729.

Fortune was never freed during his lifetime. He was one of the last slaves in Waterbury. In 1730, some 27 people were enslaved there. By 1790, that number had dropped to 12. Five were members of Fortune's family, all owned by Dr. Preserved Porter.

Author's Note

I wrote *The Manumission Requiem* soon after the events of September 11, 2001. I was hearing classical composers' requiems for the dead on public radio, and also clicking every day, as I always do, on the Hunger Site (www.hungersite.com) to donate food for the world's hungry. Every day I read on that website that about 24,000 people die each day from hunger or hunger-related causes. I decided to dedicate my requiem to everyone in the world who died on 9/11—the victims of the terrorist attacks, but also the victims of starvation, of illness, of poverty, of war, of old age, of neglect: Everyone.

My requiem has some but not all of the elements of a traditional funeral mass: the Introit (I call it a Preface), the Kyrie (the prayer of *Kyrie eleison*, Greek for "Lord, have mercy"), and the Sanctus, a hymn of praise. What is for me the high point of my requiem is "Not My Bones," which I imagined Fortune singing in his own voice. This is not part of the traditional funeral mass. When Fortune says, "You are not your body," he is quoting an ancient teaching. I learned it from Thich Nhat Hanh, the great Vietnamese Buddhist world leader, spiritual guide, and writer. After hearing him lecture, someone asked him, "What is the most helpful thing you can say to a person who is dying?" Thich Nhat Hanh replied, "We have learned, from our visits to hospices, that the most helpful thing we can say is, 'Don't worry. The body that is dying here is not you.' These words allow people to accept their deaths with peace."

A requiem, by definition, is sad; the person it honors has died. But manumission—the freeing of a slave—is a joyous event. By calling this *The Manumission Requiem*, I'm setting grief side by side with joy. I'm trying to imitate a traditional New Orleans brass band jazz funeral. When the mourners follow the body to the cemetery, they are solemn and sorrowful, and so is the music. But after the burial, after they leave the cemetery, the music becomes jubilant. The mourners dance joyfully through the streets in what they call a "second-line parade." And crowds of people, passers-by, strangers, come out and join them. What was a dirge for the dead becomes a celebration of life.

Marilyn Nelson

Fortune's Bones

THE MANUMISSION REQUIEM

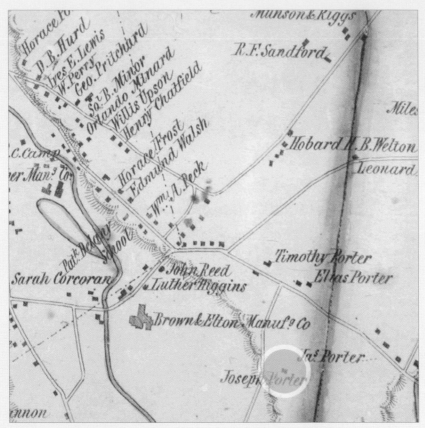

Map of Waterbury, Connecticut, from 1852, showing the location of the Porter farm.

Before Fortune was bones in a Connecticut museum, he was a husband, a father, a baptized Christian, and a slave.

His wife's name was Dinah. His sons were Africa and Jacob. His daughters were Mira and Roxa. He was baptized in an Episcopal church, which did not make him free. His master was Dr. Preserved Porter, a physician who specialized in setting broken bones.

They lived in Waterbury, Connecticut, in the late 1700s. Dr. Porter had a 75-acre farm, which Fortune probably ran. He planted and harvested corn, rye, potatoes, onions, apples, buckwheat, oats, and hay. He cared for the cattle and hogs.

Unlike many slaves, who owned little or nothing and were often separated from their families, Fortune owned a small house near Dr. Porter's home. He and Dinah and their children lived together.

Preface

Fortune was born; he died. Between those truths
stretched years of drudgery, years of pit-deep sleep
in which he hauled and lifted, dug and plowed,
glimpsing the steep impossibility
of freedom. Fortune's bones say he was strong;
they speak of cleared acres, miles of stone walls.
They say work broke his back: Before it healed,
they say, he suffered years of wrenching pain.

His wife was worth ten dollars. And their son
a hundred sixty-six. A man unmanned,
he must sometimes have waked with balled-up fists.
A white priest painted water on his head
and Fortune may or may not have believed,
whom Christ offered no respite, no reprieve,
only salvation. Fortune's legacy
was his inheritance: the hopeless hope
of a people valued for their labor, not
for their ability to watch and dream
as vees of geese define fall evening skies.
Was Fortune bitter? Was he good or bad?
Did he sometimes throw back his head and laugh?
His bones say only that he served and died,
that he was useful, even into death,
stripped of his name, his story, and his flesh.

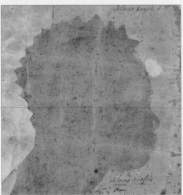

Above: Eighteenth-century silk embroidery by Prudence Punderson entitled "The First, Second and Last Scene of Mortality" (The Connecticut Historical Society, Hartford, Connecticut)
Left: No images exist of Dinah. This silhouette, traced from a candle shadow and shaded with ink, of the 19-year-old "Negro slave," Flora, was attached to Dinah's bill of sale to Asa Benjamin of Stratford dated December 13, 1796. (The Stratford [CT] Historical Society)

When Dr. Porter died in 1803, he left an estate that was worth about $7,000—a lot of money for the time. The estate included Fortune's widow, Dinah, and their son Jacob. Fortune had died in 1798.

According to Connecticut's Act of Gradual Emancipation, children born to enslaved parents after March 1, 1784, were to be freed when they reached age 21. Jacob was 18. By law, he could be enslaved for another three years.

In Dr. Porter's will, he left Dinah to his wife, Lydia. He gave Jacob to his daughter Hannah.

No one knows what happened to Africa, Mira, and Roxa.

Dinah's Lament

Miss Lydia doesn't clean the Doctor room.
She say she can't go in that room: she scared.
She make me take the dust rag and the broom
and clean around my husband, hanging there.

Since she seen Fortune head in that big pot
Miss Lydia say that room make her feel ill,
sick with the thought of boiling human broth.
I wonder how she think it make me feel?

To dust the hands what use to stroke my breast;
to dust the arms what hold me when I cried;
to dust where his soft lips were, and his chest
what curved its warm against my back at night.

Through every season, sun-up to star light,
I heft, scrub, knead: one black woman alone,
except for my children. The world so white,
nobody know my pain, but Fortune bones.

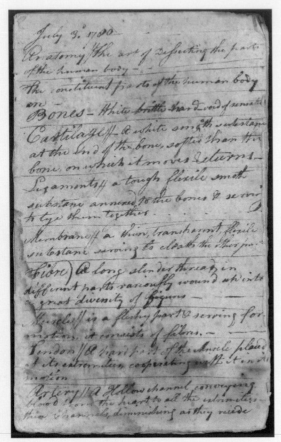

The cover page of a notebook titled "Anatomy/The Art of Dissecting the Human Body" dated July 1780.

Most slaves who died in Waterbury in the 1700s were buried in one of the town's cemeteries. When Fortune died, he wasn't buried. Instead, Dr. Porter preserved Fortune's skeleton to further the study of human anatomy.

Dr. Porter had been a bonesetter for many years, but he'd never had a skeleton to study. He had two sons who were also doctors. They could learn from the skeleton, too.

Fortune was about 60 at the time of his death and, in spite of his injuries, in relatively good health. His skeleton was sturdy and complete.

Working slowly and carefully, Dr. Porter took apart the body of his former slave. The bones were boiled to clean them of fat, and drilled to drain them of fluid. When the bones were dry, Dr. Porter identified several by inscribing them with their scientific names.

On Abrigador Hill

For fifty years my feeling hands
have practiced the bonesetter's healing touch,
a gift inherited by Porter men.
I have manipulated joints,
cracked necks, and set my neighbors back to work.
I've bled and purged fever and flux,
inoculated for smallpox,
prescribed fresh air and vegetables,
cod-liver oil and laudanum,
and closed the lightless eyes of the new dead.

And I've been humbled by ignorance,
humbled by ignorance.

Herewith begins my dissection of
the former body of my former slave,
which served him who served me throughout his life,
and now serves the advance of science.
Note well how death softens the human skin,
making it almost transparent,
so that under my reverent knife –
the first cut takes my breath away;
it feels like cutting the whole world –
it falls open like bridal gossamer.

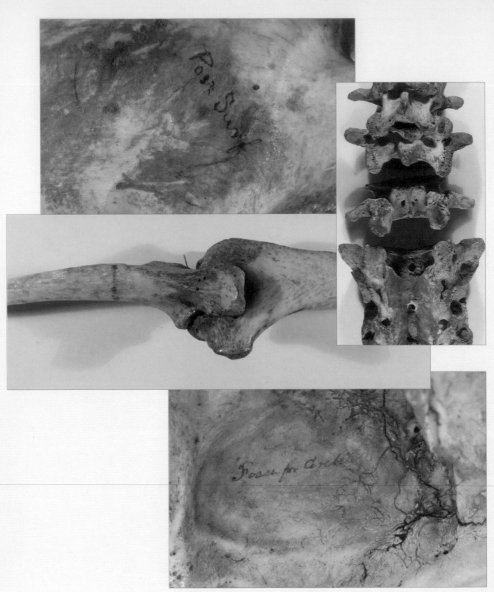

Clockwise from top left: detail of the scientific names inscribed on Fortune's scapula; tailbone, lower vertebrae; detail of the scientific names inscribed on Fortune's skull; arm bones at elbow.

Recently, when scientists examined Fortune's bones, they found that his lower back had been broken, then healed, at some time during his life. His shoulder, hands, and feet had all been injured. The study of Fortune's bones suggests that his life had been one of continuous hard labor. However, scientists do not agree completely on the cause of his death, the injuries he suffered, or the diseases he survived.

And I am humbled by ignorance,
humbled by ignorance.

Standing on a new continent
beyond the boundaries of nakedness,
I am forever changed by what I see:
the complex, delicate organs
fitted perfectly in their shelter of bones,
the striated and smooth muscles,
the beautiful integuments,
the genius-strokes of thumb and knee.
In profound and awful intimacy,
I enter Fortune, and he enters me.

And I am humbled by ignorance,
humbled by ignorance.

Dr. Jesse Porter, Preserved's son, c. 1830.

Adelia Porter Law, Preserved's granddaughter, and her son Homer, c. 1852.

Dr. Sally Porter Law McGlannan,
Preserved's great-great-granddaughter, c. 1905.

Dr. Homer Law, Preserved's
great-grandson, c. 1890.

Four more generations of Porters became physicians, and the skeleton stayed in the family. Porter children, grandchildren, and great-grandchildren used it to learn the names of the bones. This was their earliest medical training.

Sally Porter Law McGlannan, the last Porter doctor, remembered playing with the skeleton as a young girl (although no document records the story of her rolling the skull). Another family member, Leander Law, once brought part of Fortune's skeleton to a college physiology class.

At some point—no one knows exactly when—"Larry" was written on the skull. Fortune's name was forgotten for nearly a century.

Kyrie of the Bones

1800 [baritone I]

I called him Larry. It was easier
to face him with an imaginary name.
For Fortune was an image of myself:
my fortune known, my face bare bone.

[choir]

Oh, Lord, have mercy.
Gentle Jesus, have mercy.
Have mercy, Lord.

1870 [tenor]

I say he was my great-grandfather's slave,
who slipped and broke his neck on Larry's Leap.
Dispassionate and curious his gaze,
patients tell me, from the corner.

1890 [soprano]

We played in the attic on rainy afternoons:
Parcheesi, checkers. Or we took the skull
out of its wooden box, and with a leg
rolled it around the dusty floor.

John Warner Barber, Southeastern view of Waterbury, 1835

Lucien Bisbee, View of Waterbury from West Side Hill, 1837

Over the years, the skeleton was lost and found. It was boarded up in an attic, then discovered by a crew of workers hired to renovate an old building.

In 1933, Sally Porter Law McGlannan gave the bones to the Mattatuck Museum. The museum sent the bones to Europe to be assembled for display. The skeleton hung in a glass case in the museum for decades, fascinating adults and frightening children.

Many stories were invented about the skeleton. Some said that "Larry" was a Revolutionary War hero—maybe even George Washington. Some said he fell to his death. Some said he drowned. Some said he was killed trying to escape. Some thought he had been hanged.

One Waterbury resident remembers, "Larry was the thing to see when you go to the museum. I don't think anybody ever envisioned that this was truly a human being."

[choir]

Oh, Lord, have mercy.
Gentle Jesus, have mercy.
Have mercy, Lord.

1907 [tenor]

I call a hey, Luigi, come-a quick:
Look what was boarded up-a in the wall!
We stand-a with our caps over our hearts
and say an Ave Maria.

1960 [soprano]

Our field trip to the Mattatuck Museum
greatly impressed me. I'll never forget
looking into my first love's depthless eyes
right after we first saw Larry.

[choir]

Oh, Lord, have mercy.
Gentle Jesus, have mercy.
Have mercy, Lord.

Not My Bones

I was not this body,
I was not these bones.
This skeleton was just my
temporary home.
Elementary molecules converged for a breath,
then danced on beyond my individual death.
And I am not my body,
I am not my body.

We are brief incarnations,
we are clouds in clothes.
We are water respirators,
we are how earth knows.
I bore light passed on from an original flame;
while it was in my hands it was called by my name.
But I am not my body,
I am not my body.

You can own a man's body,
but you can't own his mind.
That's like making a bridle
to ride on the wind.
I will tell you one thing, and I'll tell you true:
Life's the best thing that can happen to you.
But you are not your body,
you are not your body.

Three stages of the facial reconstruction of Fortune by the forensic sculptor Frank Bender, created for the Mattatuck Museum. (Reprinted by permission of the sculptor.)

In 1970, the skeleton, still called "Larry," was taken out of its case and put into storage. Times had changed. The museum now believed that displaying the skeleton was disrespectful. It wasn't just a bunch of bones. It was the remains of someone's son, maybe someone's father.

The skeleton rested for more than 25 years. Then, in the 1990s, historians searched local records and found a slave named Fortune. Archaeologists and anthropologists studied the bones, which started giving up their secrets. The bones told how Fortune labored, suffered, and died: A quick, sudden injury, like whiplash, may have snapped a vertebra in his neck. He did not drown or fall from a cliff. He was not hanged.

But he was free.

You can own someone's body,
but the soul runs free.
It roams the night sky's
mute geometry.
You can murder hope, you can pound faith flat,
but like weeds and wildflowers, they grow right back.
For you are not your body,
you are not your body.

You are not your body,
you are not your bones.
What's essential about you
is what can't be owned.
What's essential in you is your longing to raise
your itty-bitty voice in the cosmic praise.
For you are not your body,
you are not your body.

Well, I woke up this morning just so glad to be free,
glad to be free, glad to be free.
I woke up this morning in restful peace.
For I am not my body,
I am not my bones.
I am not my body,
glory hallelujah, not my bones,
I am not my bones.

Second-line dancers at a New Orleans jazz funeral. Photograph by Leo Touchet—Woodfin Camp.

Sanctus

Holy of Holies, thy creating name
be raised above all barriers.
Each and every one of us is Fortune,
for a brief, mortal time.
Then we are compost.
Mother of all Holiness, cradle us
so we can hear the truth of your heartbeat.
Though we have wandered far, call us back home.
Eternal source of all identity,
call our true names when we forsake our bones.
Magnetic center of the universe,
make us iron filings.
Be to us what south is to autumn geese.
Call us home, Lord, call us home.
Call us home, Lord, set us free.

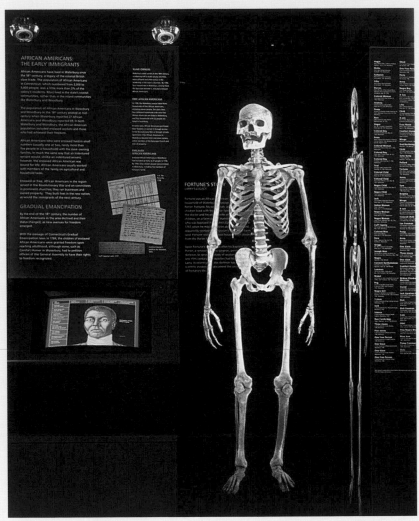

The "Fortune's Story/Larry's Legacy" exhibit kiosk at the Mattatuck Museum. This permanent, interactive exhibit opened to the public on March 29, 2003.

Afterword

The Manumission Requiem was commissioned by the Mattatuck Museum after a three-year process to recover Fortune's history. A team of anthropologists, archaeologists, and historians, working with the museum's staff, have given us new insights into local history and slavery in Connecticut through their study of Fortune's bones and historical documents. Their work forms the basis for most of the historical notes that accompany the requiem, as well as an exhibit and website at the museum.

This has been a community-based project from its beginning. The museum's African American History Project committee, serving as a liaison with the public, met with the researchers to consider the implications of the new insights, issues, and discoveries of Fortune's life and the possible causes of his death.

When the Fortune Project began, the committee members felt strongly that Fortune's remains should be buried. Now they are divided on this issue, as are visitors to the museum's exhibit "Fortune's Story/Larry's Legacy." Fortune's bones were preserved by Dr. Porter to teach human anatomy. Many members of the African American History Project Committee believe that Fortune has more to teach us still. Others feel strongly that it is time to rest his bones in consecrated ground.

As the project continues, new developments in the story will be posted on our website, www.FortuneStory.org.

Marie Galbraith
Executive Director, Mattatuck Museum
Waterbury, Connecticut

Notes and Sources

Jacket and page 24: The painting of Fortune, based on his skeleton (see the photograph on page 2), is by medical illustrator William Westwood and is printed with the artist's permission. Page 6 is an overlay of the photograph of Fortune's skelton and Westwood's painting.

Title page: Bill of sale for a slave named Peter, who was sold to Edward Hinman of Woodbury, CT, in 1762. It is in the collection of the Mattatuck Museum.

The quotation, "Larry was the thing to see…," on page 22 is from "Hidden Museum Treasures: Fortune's Bones: 18th-Century Slave Gets New Life, New Recognition," heard on National Public Radio's *All Things Considered*, September 16, 2003.

The photograph on page 28 is from *Rejoice When You Die: The New Orleans Jazz Funerals*. Photographs by Leo Touchet, text by Vernel Bagneris, introduction by Ellis L. Marsalis, Jr. Baton Rouge, LA: Louisiana State University Press, 1998, p. 132-133.

Dugdale, Antony, J.J. Fueser, and J. Celso de Castro Alves. "Yale, Slavery and Abolition." Copyright © 2001 by The Amistad Committee, Inc., New Haven, CT. www.yaleslavery.org.

Harper, Douglas. "Slavery in Connecticut," from "Slavery in the North." www.slavenorth.com/connecticut.htm.

Lang, Joel. "The Skeleton in the Closet." From *Complicity: How Connecticut Chained Itself to Slavery*, a special issue of *Northeast*, the Sunday magazine of the *Hartford Courant*. September 29, 2002, p. 71.

"Fortune's Story/Larry's Legacy." A permanent exhibit at the Mattatuck Museum, 144 West Main Street, Waterbury, CT 06702.

Unpublished documents in the archive of the Mattatuck Museum.